The King's Touch

Also by Tom Sleigh

THE KING'S TOUCH

Poems

Tom Sleigh

Graywolf Press

This publication is made possible, in part, by the voters of Minnesota through a Minnesota State Arts Board Operating Support grant, thanks to a legislative appropriation from the arts and cultural heritage fund. Significant support has also been provided by Target Foundation, the McKnight Foundation, the Lannan Foundation, the Amazon Literary Partnership, and other generous contributions from foundations, corporations, and individuals. To these organizations and individuals we offer our heartfelt thanks.

Published by Graywolf Press
250 Third Avenue North, Suite 600
Minneapolis, Minnesota 55401

www.graywolfpress.org

Published in the United States of America

ISBN 978-1-64445-077-2

2 4 6 8 9 7 5 3 1
First Graywolf Printing, 2022

Library of Congress Control Number: 2021940563

Cover design: Kyle G. Hunter

Cover art: *James VI and I (1566–1625)*, c. 1620. After Paul van Somer. Oil on canvas. Photograph by Mike Davidson. From the Royal Collection Trust. Fingerprint and wildfire images from iStock.

Contents

III

IV

High cries were felled and a pure change happened.

—Seamus Heaney

The King's Touch

I

Youth

Smelling of sweet resin the Aleppo pines'
shadows grow taller by the hour. Two identical
twin boys chase each other through the shadows,
the one who's ten minutes older yelling,
"I'm gonna kill you!" while the younger one
laughs, "Kill me, kill me if you can!"
Day by day these teatime mortars
keep pecking at the blast wall but the boys
have grown so used to it they keep on playing.
If they weren't here in front of me, I'd find them
hard to imagine, just as I sometimes find
my own twin brother hard to imagine.
I'm supposed to be doing a story
on soldiers, what they do to keep from
being frightened, but all I can think about
is how Tim would chase me or I'd chase him
and we'd yell, "I'm gonna kill you," just like
these brothers do, so alive in their bodies,
just as Tim who is so alive will one day not be:
will it be me or him who first dies?
But I came here to do a story on soldiers
and how they keep watching out for death
and manage to fight and die without going crazy—
the boys squat down to look at ants climbing
through corrugated bark, the wavering antennae
tapping up and down the tree reminding me
of the soldier across the barracks sitting
still inside himself, listening to his nerves
while his eyes peer out at something I can't see—
when Achilles' immortal mother came
to her grieving son, knowing he would soon
die, and gave him his armor and kept the worms

from the wounds of his dead friend, Patroclus, she,
a goddess, knew she wouldn't be allowed
to keep those same worms from her son's body.

I know I'm not his father, he's not my son,
but he looks so young, young enough to be
my son—sitting on his bunk, watching out for death,
trying to fight and die without going crazy, he
reaches for his rifle, breaks it down,
dustcover, spring, bolt carrier with piston,
wiping it all down with a rag and oil,
cleaning it for the second time this hour
while shadows shifting through the pines
bury him and the little boys and Tim
and me as I'm supposed to be doing a story
in nonmetaphorical, real-life darkness.

In Which a Spider Weaves a Web
on My Computer Screen

1

What is that shadow that weaves itself so fine
across the edge of my computer screen?
There it is, a pinprick of a spider weaving
a web I'm looking through, as if it were a veil of second
sight that, as I type these words behind
the veil, the screenlight shines right through.

It weaves the sun into its web and turns
the screen into a mirror shooting back
my own eyes looking at the spider
and wondering what the spider knows of me.
Hello, pal, I want to say, but that feels
unctuous, overly familiar for what I know

I'm going to do. The web sways
and ripples each time I breathe, getting ready
to rip it away. There's a lot of casual brutality
to reconcile. The spider clings to its web's outer rim,
plucks with a slender leg a near-invisible guy-wire
each time I type a word and the silk trembles.

2

He said that being a refugee was like living like a spider
in the bottom of a well. He held his quiet dignity
close to him. The others in the room stopped talking.

I won't repeat exactly what he said since it's his
to tell. But it had to do with how his mother died,
how his home was destroyed. The words you use

to talk about such things, the second they're
uttered, sound suspect. For him to say, "The soldiers
shot my father, they blew up our house, and the worst

thing I ever saw, the very worst, was seeing my baby
brother crying on my dead mother's breast"
is only my rendering in English what the translator

speaking in French said he said. Raveled in
words as a spider is raveled in its silk, I think
I should know what to want to say but to want

to say is not what the man in his use of a figure
of a spider drifting suspended, tethered
to a lifeline spinning out impossibly fine, intends

when he says, "The deeds to my house are stained
with blood," and then shows you the stains, three long stains
dried brown and fading above the signature line.

"refugee"

1

It makes a difference to the refugees
to leave today rather than tomorrow—

the sooner the gate of the camp shuts behind them
and the world lies all before them
and where to choose their place of rest

the sooner they can spit out the taste of "refugee."

2

Hail to the conquerors who soon enough
will be refugees from the earth.

Hail to the earth that never gave a damn about them,
the conquerors or the conquered, one hunching

behind his tanks, thinking he's advancing
by driving the others stumbling in front of him,

while both are being herded by the Invisible—
the Invisible that doesn't see them except at the very second

they disappear from sight like a bullet tunneling
underwater, leaving a bull's-eye of ripples

widening all the way to the horizon.

3

Will dates
carved in slate
being worn away
by wind and rain
outlast our
always-disappearing species?

If you adjust your ears
to the proper frequency,
you can hear
our bones
in marked and unmarked graves
talk among themselves, rehearsing
cold facts
about who never passed the test
of standing up
on two legs,
who never left
the savannah for the forest,
who hemmed and hawed over whether God exists.

4

The dead buried in sand
stare up through thornbushes' roots.
Underneath them,
floor by floor
as in a stone tenement
that sinks down
to the center
of the earth,
the dead,
old and young,

rich, poor,
those without hope
and the hopelessly lonely,
whisper quietly to the living,
Goodbye, Homo sapiens, goodbye.

5

Look at us, an entire species
crowding into marble lobbies where
the eternal doormen shimmer in uniforms of dust.

They don't hand us the mail or ask us how we are.
They don't even stare when we too turn to dust
and the wind
begins to blow us into dunes
across a desert so wide that the distance
between each grain of sand
keeps halving itself the instant we reach halfway
so that no matter how close we come
home's always far away.

6

The face of Zeno
driven from home
curses the paradox
that bears his name.

He lives in the desert
as we do.
Only the desert

is his mind
that refutes blood and bone

the instant the tortoise sets out on his race
with a head start on Achilles
who comes racing after him
but always just behind
the tortoise
because no matter how quickly Achilles runs,
the tortoise in that time
crawls a little farther
and so always it's just ahead
and keeps on going long after
Achilles runs out of breath.

From hour to hour
we run
but we never catch up
to the tortoise's shadow.

7

I was thirsty the day I was born
and wailed for milk, mother, water, sun.

The sun hunkered down
at the only borehole in the desert
and waited for me to get big enough
to crawl to the edge
of old age and climb over.

Not-Her

"Just a child" is the phrase for them the NGOers always used.
A phrase in which "just a child" meant categories
of inviolable trust, of innocence destroyed, of abused

understandings between NGOers, parents, child, world.
But when I stepped back, and I was, in my role,
as overly involved in assuming what she was—"murdered"—

as anyone, I saw it all from a space-time continuum
not hers—and that was when I had to back off and try to see
it clear: the not-her who was not her file in Refugee Protection

and who, in some otherworld parallel to this one,
kept on staring over my shoulder as I read about
the murders of her, her father, and brothers by gunmen

who came into their house and asked them
all to step into the street where in a businesslike way,
in the back of the head, they gunned them down.

While her not-her looked on, I looked at violated
trust, innocence investigated, disabused
understandings between tribe and tribe, Mohammed

and Jesus, nation and nation, each examining her forensics:
"round contact wound with blackened seared
skin margins, lead snowstorm appearance

on X-ray due to peeling back of bullet jacket releasing
minute lead fragments, radiating
fractures of occipital bone . . ." Almost nothing

to go on except the fact that she was in the database
the Protection woman showed me: "This," she said,
"is what makes my job difficult." But now that she was

not-her, did not-her need no protecting,
not just-a-child, not tooth-for-tooth, snowstorm, Mohammed,
Jesus, not-even-a-picture-of-her-living?

Bernini's *David* as a Young Man with a Slingstone and an Electronics Repair Shop

Scraped bare ground, blockade by sea,
body quarried out of stone winding up
to let the slingstone fly

toward the radar dish's giant eye hidden
behind the berm where soldiers in tanks
fire at him. His face turns

to an image multiplied in cellphone
eyes he brushes by
when he crosses into the No Go Zone,

tear gas smelling of battery acid and sour lilies:
call him what you want, smash him
with a hammer, imagine he's

Juan Marichal high-kicking
into his wind-up, pitching a no-hitter
for the Giants in 1963, his marble mouth clenching,

eyes narrowing as he aims his slingstone
whirling round and round. But now he fights free
of the marble, he slips beyond the frame

his maker chiseled for him, he motions me to write down,
I'm twenty-seven years old, I have a wife
and two sons and I welcome you to my home:

he puts on magnifying goggles to see the broken
circuit board, the solder going molten,
flux smoking up from the beading join.

—Bernini lived in the 1600s but knew nothing
of Italy, there were no Italians, he was
a Roman who chiseled fingers gripping

marble flesh so real the fingertips
press deep into the stone. You can talk
all you want about turning into a symbol, you can keep

rehearsing the droning
violence of a star, its atonal music
of the spheres stopping the planets from colliding.

But what he does as a young man,
what David did as shepherd or king,
what soldiers or cellphones

want from him now, can't make the stone
know him or stop it flying from the sling,
aimed like a probe beyond the sun.

Confession

Everything they said, reasonable, thought through,
moved like maggots on the carcass of a dog—
the dog's flesh crawled with an intelligence
of its own while those maggots declaimed
the higher virtues of the high-minded
Oppression Freedom Freedom from Oppression Law
Order Law and Order Dialectics
of the Dispossessed—
                              but out in the street
where the crowd was shouting, and some guy
had his elbow stuck into my ear, and the cops
on the walkie-talkie were starting to freak out,
calling in reinforcements while a young man
with a bullhorn balanced on the hood
of somebody's car, *Come on come on*
let's rush them, and the pressure of the crowd
began to crush me, I felt myself float up
and hover above your city:
                              street on street
of apartments sagging from the shelling,
roofs caved in, whole walls sheared away
looking like dollhouses you can see inside,
a sofa and chairs half-buried under plaster,
a kitchen table with plates still on it,
a picture of the Prophet knocked askew.
My aspiring martyr, remember
the air-conditioners' chill oases
in the hard-partying cafés that are now rubble?
By now, the sea has soaked your heart through.

Now you can speak the dry-mouthed truth
of tear gas still clinging to your T-shirt as you smile
at me from the screen and say with a shy shrug,
as if you were confessing some small fault,
"Tom, all my friends and my enemies' friends are dead."

Up the Hill

Love is nothing but a mattress made of needles.
The young soldier on guard stops me from climbing
any higher up the hill, he points me the way back down
along a track of barbwire and overgrown flowering vines
wreathing the wire as a kind of trellis.
But before I turn around, I offer him a cigarette,
and we stand there, smoking.
He doesn't ask me anything, and since I don't speak
his language, we look first at each other,
then squint down at the sea
funneling the rich, briny, low-tide muck mixed with sewage, diesel.

On top of the hill, in a little sandbagged,
corrugated tin hut, the off-duty sentry
lies sleeping on his side on a slab of cardboard
from a packing box.
The language
feels too heavy in my ears until I see
the smoothness, where the hair stops growing
on the back of his neck, roughen
to the little battleground of red welts
where mosquitos have bitten him just below his collar.

The sleeping soldier pulls his knees
up to his chest: he could be you, reader, or me—
one of us drawing the other one close, yours or my chest
warm against the other's shoulder blades
that you or I say, in a low voice, feel so good, so sharp.

Reading

1

Nodding off over your gun,
you sleep an hour, a year, you're erasing
yourself moment by moment until you're just your outline.
What was the name of the village boy scrounging

from the bush war a shattered TV screen?
He held the screen up so it framed his face as he
announced, "This is the news," calling it *Kid TV.*
In the armored vehicle circling round

and round, you scribble in your notebook "A Last Note"
to your mother or try to read *Petals
of Blood* or stare up at Patrice's uniformed butt

as he mans the machine gun, his helmet
exposed, his sights trained on the market
slapping in your faces its raw-meat smell.

2

You feel that little spike of tension
when the barrel of a gun swivels in your direction
and asks you for your passport and intentions.

Every chance you've ever taken, telling yourself
it's all OK until it's not OK and then it's too late,
won't let you turn back now.

Famine, starvation, war—
you see yourself high up
as if you were staring

down at the shadow of the wing
passing over sand, date palms, salt-whitened hardpan,
the chott pulsing with heat waves

as you feel that little buckling in the self, obedient,
subjugate, already a little spent
before the fighting has even begun.

And then you think of the soldier reading in his bunk
who doesn't bother to look up
when the mortar rounds begin to land.

3

You read how first there was reading
that opened his eyes to the pit
he was in but with no ladder to climb out.

Then how his copybook was a wooden fence,
brick wall, pavement, his pen and ink
a lump of chalk, his instructors the ship carpenters

writing on ship timbers *L* for *larboard*,
S for *starboard*. With these, he learns to write—
but then finds himself regretting his own existence

and wishing he were dead; and but for
the hope of being free, "I have
no doubt that I should have killed

myself or done something for which I
should have been killed."
Or think of that other one who, when alone,

would talk to "my book and put my ear to it
in hopes it would answer. And I have been
much concerned when it remained silent."

All those years you believed that books
would sustain you through sickness, war,
while age and race walked on your face—

who you were, who you are, the color
of your skin, the reckoning of being
just one person day after day, suddenly gives way

to this sunlit isolation before going into action, crossing
the frontier into the frontier of writing
where all you can hear is a flat voice asking,

"How can you reconcile, age after age, the man
who writes 'all men are created equal'
and then sells a slave to buy new books?"

4

"In the punishment cell
they feed you a handful of dry gruel,
so dry you have to mix it
with toothpaste
to get it down.
Even your last meal
is subject to apartheid.
Before being
hanged, the white
prisoner gets a whole
roast chicken,
the black prisoner
gets half.
Strangely enough,
from the time they're
condemned, blacks
get the same food
as whites—
except for that last meal.
It's like a kind of
reaffirmation
of apartheid in
the final
moment before
the gallows.

If my mother's letters
had more than the number
of words allowed,
the prison censor

got a kick out of waving the letter
in front of me
and counting the number
of excess words
he'd cut, just snipped
off the end.
            And when
my mother died,
I was given no privacy
to cry—
the guards just stared at me
constantly to watch
my reaction."

5

When your car leaves the border for a back road
so dim you can barely see your hand,
the tarmac keeps almost coming to an end

as you hear the fluttering of pages
torn from a book that keep blowing out
the rolled-down window's polished dark.

Driving on and on, when evening brings
"the death loneliness that haunts
the end of each and every day,"

you remember a man who came home
to his study, changed the clothes he'd worn to work
covered now in mud and dirt,

and put on his only suit and tie,
the clothes he wore each night to enter
the palace and court of the great learned dead

where courteously received by them, he fed
himself on that food that was his alone and for which he was born,
unashamed to talk with them and ask

about the reasons behind their lives, and that they,
out of human kindness, were glad to answer.
I read almost all night how for hours at a time

this man felt no boredom, he forgot his problems,
he didn't dread being poor and wasn't scared of dying.
I read how he read to forget himself completely.

6

Think of Ms. Toshiko Sasaki working at the tin factory
when the blast wave hurls on top of her a wall
of books that first instant of the atomic age—

but somehow she survives
to read another day, her world
reduced to the shadow of a ladder

and a man getting ready to climb rung after rung
to the nowhere etched forever up the wall.
And in my own private twilight zone, how can I deny

the bookworm bank teller reading in the bank vault
during his lunch hour—
the same hour as Armageddon.

But the sun still shines on a world whose still point
is the lone survivor reading, no longer thinking
about the rubble, at least for as long as the book lasts.

Up the library steps and under the glass dome
to where I sat watching the readers staring
at the paper glaring like salt flats from which letters

in a buzzing black swarm rose up,
whoever from that gone world still keeps on
keeps moving their mouths to show me

how to move mine, my eyes tracking
their eyes down the page
in what my mother calls "reading"—

like a voice talking but it's inside your head
telling you a story until you feel yourself set loose,
swept up into vowel into consonant into vowel,

so that my first things will also be my last,
the page turning and the page
just turned keeping the world spinning.

A Dictator Walks into a Bar

In the hotel lobby, leaning against a marble column
from when the Romans ruled, I sip my vodka as gunfire
night and day ricochets in celebration

punctuating someone's wedding or a moment in
someone's mood in which blowing
off a clip into the air fights off boredom:

in this cell-phone video that's more slashes of light,
jiggle and jag than a stable point of view,
I watch them drag him from muck out of a culvert,

his kufi knocked askew, heavy body thrown
across a Toyota battlewagon
where an electrical engineer turned militiaman,

who reminds me of my father, mild, unshowy,
studiously polite, doesn't smile, frown, as he
watches himself slapping, in the footage that he's

showing me, the Brother Leader, great Murshid,
the Guide—doesn't comment, doesn't shy away
from my oh-so-fine-tuned sensitivities

quivering on the brink, maybe a little drunk, my cloak of objectivity
already tattering into rags—his lumps, welts
not quite bleeding—unable to look away,

am I hoping to see blood? It isn't every day that a dictator writhes
under your heel—the one powerful enough to say,
Those who do not love me do not deserve to live—

as if he himself were the soul in the body politic and we
were just an afterthought, accessory
to his glory, the merest janitors to his trash, or maybe

just the trash itself, all of us human trash waiting
to be burned. But now, it's our turn,
and we've got him where we want him—

his livid puffy face, its blankness unto death
like slopped-over paint running down the can—
his nose by now smashed in so his mouth

hangs open to the blahness of desert hardpan and cliffs shadowing
tank tracks back into the Nafusa Mountains
where just an hour ago we were driving and he was worrying

about load-shedding and high-voltage grids,
the tragedy of no infrastructure—while I was daydreaming
of vodka and peeling happy-hour shrimp

glinting like armor plate—finally, I've seen enough; but as I
turn to give him back his phone he's moved down
the bar and seems, head bowed, to be

peering into his drink with that intimate anticipation
that could signal a joke or a prayer speeding
to its punchline, only it's the new kind

of humor, the new kind of prayer
in which the jokes aren't funny and prayers don't deliver,
and whether you're praying or laughing, it's all on you.

Fly

Whatever his Excellency may say about "the situation," "the long-term
    outlook,"
I'm only a fly buzzing around his head. Concerned with breeding, feeding,
    my outlook
decidedly short term. It's so hard to be cornered forever in a human
    form . . . now I see

everything from a hundred different angles in a thousand different lenses.
Other signs to parse: power is his Excellency's insignia, I can hear it
    breathing his lungs in and out
as if he were being kept alive on a ventilator.

That's how you know when whatever is 100 percent in a person takes over
    every thought, every moment.
Power is never less than 100 percent.
How do you escape it, how do you keep from being stalled forever, each
    filament inside you glowing like a heater

in a room that gets just so warm and no warmer?
You have to grow wings, you have to accept that roadkill is your meat,
    you have to risk being crushed by a flailing hand.
But once you do, you can train each of your lenses on the tiny worlds

taking place in each of your eyes, worlds where the Excellencies are just
    another flaw in the rock crystal
dissolving under the force of the giant waterfall, the Iguazu Falls,
that only a fly can cross, borne through mist by mist.

II

Dream of a Song Woven from the Veil

The Song I dream of isn't Jeanie
with the light brown hair but more the eyes

of the shaman flying beyond his body toward *spiritus mundi*
but finding there a wall spray-painted FREE MUMIA

ICH BIN EIN BERLINER
IF YOU CAN READ THIS YOUR MAMA IS A WHORE

while a boombox archaic as Linear B
blasts Cannonball and Nat playing "Mercy, Mercy, Mercy."

Some teenage acolyte longing to be Nat
learns his part slavish note by note,

loving Nat's attack on the bridge before the chorus
while past boarded-up row houses the last city bus

drives through the elegiac whine
of razor wire whistling when all the sirens drown.

As marines at the USO club at Pendleton shout
with our horn section in the onslaught

of mercy begged for in the valley of B-flat,
I heard echo beyond the spotlight

our band's mayhem torturing the Song
that no matter how off-key we play refuses to lie down

with the shadows of the grunts dancing on their own; and I see
through the Veil mine own Mr. Curdy,

my avatar, my teacher, whose perfect pitch
when we play duets tears the Veil to bits,

my tone wavering in and out of tune as we purse
our lips in the learned kiss of our embouchures.

But it's more than just a Song woven from the Veil—
it's a live, bent grammar just coming into being, a viral

sadness in choruses passed around
in smoke-filled air filling up with variations

on flying rocks and bottles, cruisers set on fire,
everybody running while the camera pans after

in this most personal of shoot-outs
between sax and cornet

played by the brothers in dueling overtones
digging under the skin of the tune being born.

Dead Me, Live Me

When you told me how the reindeer people thought the world

of the dead is the mirror image of the living
and the ground is the surface of the mirror,
I thought how the me who walks on Smith Street
is just the right-side-upness of my dead me's

upside-downness, his feet matching mine
step for step, sole to sole. But the reindeer people
are dying out. And once they're gone,
will both worlds shatter and disappear?

When I think of going down without you and never

coming back up, I remember descending
stone stairs spiraling and narrowing
until the people in front of me and those in back
had to fall in line behind each other so we

entered single file what seemed the bottom
of a well but was a burial chamber
where limestone shaped into a giant scallop shell
held the bodies of two babies, stillborn.

The skins of two martens, cream and brown fur

still sleek under a transparent sheet of calcite,
glistened on top of them; a wild boar's foreleg
was laid across their shoulders; a withered
human foot had been placed between their feet;

the blackened shells of eighty-six tortoises
gleamed around them, and an aurochs tail nestled
along their spines. Poor live me, dependent on memory
to survive, knows one day he'll be dead me without you.

We're naked. We've grown old. We doze off in each other's arms.

Migration

The wild, profane grandma is embarrassing the grandson:
he chokes up on his bat, he knocks anxious dirt off his cleats,

he looks up and down the diamond
as if looking for a place to hide: listen to her shouting,

Come on, boy, come on, hit that ball right outta here—
her face swaddled by a sun mask so only her eyes show,

she's the mummy in the movie that chases down
the pretty girl, she's the silence after the movie

when he hunches in his bed, covers pulled up over his head,
unmoving, sweating, chewing on his pajama collar, spit

tasting of fear, thinking, Is that
the monster coming? But now, here, in the light,

for her sake, his sake, for the team's sake, the boy would like her
to be quiet, not actually to shut up, but quiet down—

one strike, two strikes—*Hey, batter batter batter batter, swing!*
He's walking back to the bench, his head hung down:

and she's watching him, her eyes OK and not OK with it,
Hey, good cut, good swing, always go down swinging—

he puts his bat in the rack as he's been taught,
and whatever his thoughts are or her thoughts, whatever

either one is feeling, she behind her mask, he
pulling his cap down so you can't see his eyes, remains hidden

from the other—but if you were to saw open their skulls,
if you were to dissect the walnut-shaped amygdala

where all this feeling is electrical signals firing,
what you'd see are nerve fibers, long strands of tissue

that look like dead people's hair braided into amulets, lockets
in barrows and old tombs: you'd see little lightning storms

of rising glare, you'd see it all as pure physical phenomena—
no allegory or interpretation of emotion

of ashamed grandson and crazy grandma
still shouting through his unease, *Come on, Wolfpack,*

shut 'em down, shut 'em down . . . no, all you'd see
would be these staticky flashes of electrons signaling

to the brain image on image imposed one
upon another in minute detail, seen as from far away,

high up in the clouds: but then this dance of the earth
sponsored by Ace Hardware and Paul's Auto Body

would be, as you plunged into it, magnified through your lenses
to huge white expanses—and there they'd be,

these little tiny beings in all that blizzard whiteness
struggling along, as if falling behind some annual migration

though the reason for it is lost, the significance
and bearing on the tribal life is gone.

False Teeth

i.m. Pauline Thyfault

After the viewing, they took her new false teeth,
inhumanly gleaming, out of her mouth, then slid
her body in the oven and turned up the flame.
They offered them to me as "a keepsake,
a remembrance" but I turned them down:
all I wanted to see, all I wanted
to remember was the old wrecked acropolis
of her shattered grin. She, whose soul had been
tight-jawed, gap-toothed, a cavity-drilled
dissenter, possessed in her new dentures
the permanent reminder of how all those years
she'd hidden her shamed smile. It was as if
the porcelain grins of the ones she called
the bosses, and hated with the purity
of a blowtorch cutting steel, had become her grin
mocking her from the water glass she soaked
them in at night, their perfect alignment
and corrected overbite become my little
nightmare, gnashing, tearing, hyperbolic
in their appetite, as if they embodied
hunger stripped of any satisfaction,
the anti-food of hunger hungering
to eat and eat never stopping, chewing
the void between each tooth to the least
nano of a nothing. Once, when I went
to see her and she still recalled her name,
I saw her staring at those teeth, saying
something like *gobble gobble gobble* but might
have been her mumbling nonsense syllables
while those teeth faced her down, square and perfect,
no jaw or skull to detract from their exactness,
knowing nothing of all her years driving Jersey's

backcountry roads checking in on what she
called God's beloved crazies though she didn't
believe in God, nor did she see them as crazy—
the social services lady who went house
to house and got Millie out of her locked room,
took Arthur to a matinee where he pissed himself
and she had to clean him up in the men's
while the teenage ushers looked the other way.
Once she drove me to an abandoned house where
a dentist had his surgery, the chair still there,
kapok on the floor, even the little pedal
he pumped with his foot to drive the drill,
windows broken, stained posters of dancing
gleaming teeth as a hand without an arm
brushes that smile to little sparkles
leaping from too-pink gums. Just why or what
we did fades into my looking into
her mouth, at the wildly spaced voids between
each tooth as she talked to another lady;
but if you think I'm going to tell you
what I saw, play the little boy smitten
with the flawed, go back and read again:
I said nothing about her smile being
anything but a cause of shame, nothing
about a husband, a child, a female lover,
though she lived with a woman named Joy
who brought her anything but, haranguing her
in old age to change and change again
her paltry will. Instead, her dream of overcoming
the rich for the kingdom of the poor
all those years she hid her teeth behind her hand
vanished in one instant of these new damned teeth
that make everything taste like metal, as straight
and even as these pretty-boy newscasters
shoving their perfect mugs into your face.

Black Dog, White Dog

The souls of the dead wake up and bark at the living,
they whine and leap, they slowly settle down into dogs' bodies,
human time ticks away until it no longer rushes in their ears,
the dead souls leap up with muddy paws
and live in the moment of their leaping.

Into fangs, claws, nostrils, into wriggles
of excitement as they sniff rot rising from gutters
where wonders of the invisible turn visible in their nostrils,
black dog, white dog, they are where the souls go.

Play-fighting in the grass, each nip an invitation
to further provocation, they squirm round to face the other's jaws,
lunging for an opening beneath the other's throat.

Ask me whose dog I am bleeding in the dream,
ask me why my master's voice spreads cell by cell,
ask yourself whose soul is barking at you now,
and whose SIT GODDAMN IT SIT lashes in your ears.

Through the eternal afternoon, black fur, white fur keep on playing,
lie down together, one's head cradled on the other's back
lazily rolling over, offering up its soft belly to the other.

Words from Chernobyl

"The sun beat down on me, birds were nesting, graves
were being dug. The army gave us gloves,
respirators, surgical robes. The sun
beat down on us, we were living in
this parallel, not-Earth world where the Apocalypse
met the Stone Age. We were trolls, demons
showing up in people's yards, and our job was
to bury everything—bugs, spiders, worms,

all colors, all killed by hundreds, thousands—we rolled
them all up in big plastic sheets,
not knowing what they were called,
these bugs, spiders, worms, destroying their houses, secrets.
And we buried them: including the soil we buried in the soil, earth to earth:
and that's what I remember most, burying
the bugs, spiders, leeches . . . When they sent me there in spring,
birds were nesting, everything was giving birth,

the place was so awful because it was so beautiful—
and when they let me leave, radioactive apples
glowed against the snow. They told us we had to win
but against what? Physics, the universe, the atom . . . ?
There's a parable about a guy who lived in Jerusalem
and Christ was staggering right past his home,
he watched him collapse under the cross and cry out.
He saw all this, but his tooth hurt,

so he didn't run outside. And two days later, when
his tooth stopped hurting, people told him,
Christ! Christ has risen! And he thought:
I could have been a witness to it—but my tooth hurt.
So is that how it always is? One minute

ants are crawling along a branch, the sun beats down on it,
it's just your average chaos, and the next
it's why don't you all go fuck yourselves?

My dad defended Moscow in 1942. But it was only through
books and movies he found too tedious to finish
that he realized years later what he'd been through—
his own memory of the 'great event' was:
'I sat in a trench. Shot my rifle. Got
buried by an explosion. They dug me out
half-alive.' That's it. My dad liked to say that people shoot
but it's God who guides the bullet."

After a Sentence in a Letter from Pasternak to Rilke, 1926

"The revolution is a tourist attraction"
writes Pasternak to Rilke just as Rilke,
feeling ill, but not yet knowing he's dying
of leukemia, pages through a catalog,
ordering soft white nightshirts and a woolen shawl.
While Tsvetaeva, part of this epistolary threesome,
writes to Rilke, "I love you and want to sleep
with you; friendship does not allow brevity."
But Rilke, who's never met her, prefers
the mail and masturbation—and writes her
two more letters before he drops her
for his final girlfriend and her sports car
taking mountain curves in Switzerland
at 90 miles an hour—while his most faithful
lover, his long-time doctor, cares like
a sister for the raw black pustules
breaking out across his skin until, just after
Christmas, 1926, he literally
dies in his doctor's arms, eyes open.
So much for Orpheus climbing back from
the underworld. So much for Tsvetaeva
as Eurydice, who kills herself in 1942,
writing in her final hours on a broken-backed
table three letters she weighed down with
a little zip Parisian handbag
she loved to swing in circles in the air:
the first for the person who will find her hanging
from the stairwell just outside her door;
the second to a poet friend begging him to take care
of her son and a trunk full of her own poems,
which of course he refuses, too fearful
that he and his family will be arrested;

the last to her sixteen-year-old son, who will soon
be drafted and killed in the war, telling him,
"I love you . . . but I've come to a dead-end street."

Pasternak outlives them both while all around him
his friends are arrested, kill themselves, waste away
from typhus, dysentery, or freeze to death
in a transport train to the work camps.
One thousand five hundred writers
of his generation are murdered: all it takes
is an anonymous denunciation, a system
so pernicious that another poet's wife,
who of course outlives her husband, tells
the story of how the head of her department
in the college in which she's teaching calls
a special meeting to plead with his colleagues
to stop denouncing each other—the paperwork,
the paperwork alone! is killing him!

The revolution is a tourist attraction
like the Cyclone at Coney Island—
Tsvetaeva and Pasternak, with Rilke
wedged between them in the very first car,
feel the chain tauten as they cling to the bar,
the wooden track angling so steeply upward
all they see is dizzying sky—and now they approach
the plunge, lifted into a motionless still
balance in the air, the threesome yet one,
then falling, crashing, sucked under in a roar
that inundates them forever . . . The revolution
thunders over them, even over Rilke
who writes enthusiastically of Lenin's
eloquence, but also of Mussolini's,
not hearing in his lofty castle the fist
knocking on the apartment door at two a.m.—

a young man eager to ascend the ranks
who pushes his way past you and begins to search
your tiny room, throwing your clothes
on the floor and deliberately trampling
on them, enraged and astonished at how
many pairs of socks you have, at the sheer
beauty of the colors, socks that make him
want to beat you and burst into tears,
and underwear without holes and freshly laundered.

Oh Pasternak, Tsvetaeva, we know the Russians
are coming, the Russians are always coming, they're like
those barbarians that are a kind of solution:
purges, imprisonments, massacres . . . and all of us
the heirs of Rilke's boundlessness, his knowledge
of death as life's greatest dimension,
the mountains of primal grief unreachable
even in a sports car . . . but the dimensions
of the prisons keep widening and widening
until they close in on us, on some ordinary Olga—
Pasternak's lover going to prison because she won't
inform on him while around her people starve
and die of exhaustion in the camp's wooden huts
where the water basin hardens into ice overnight
and Pasternak can do nothing but keep on
writing his novel in which she is the heroine—
Pasternak, who could have been killed, should
have been killed for refusing to sign an open letter
condemning Marshal Tukhachevsky, and then
explained his reasons to the man who'd
insisted he sign, who said, "Borya, you're
a good man, a saintly man," embraced him
with both arms, and then went straight to the secret police
and denounced him. And so Pasternak calls
his country a slave ship in which the Party overseers

whip the rowers: so why wasn't he pulled
from bed in his pajamas, his overcoat hung
carefully by the door next to a little suitcase
already packed since everyone knew that one day
they'd be taken to Lubyanka to be beaten
and forgotten, signing a confession that no one
would even read? And yet he survived . . . and the reason
is that Stalin, on a whim? as a little joke
to himself? scribbled in the poet's file,
Let this little cloud-dweller keep on living among his clouds.

Practice Range
Erbil, Kurdistan

1

Before me on the screen the masked soldier
sings in Arabic, "Shining bright as jewels in a bride's
ear, our tanks will destroy the unbeliever."

In the desert background, wind keeps
stirring up the dust as the singer, an AK
slung over his shoulder, mocks

"the deputy sheiks of Google who preach jihad,
but all they do is click on the top right corner."
And there's the widow singing, "All my men are dead—"

grieving for sons and husband: "Yesterday
was cheerful, lively, but today
the world abandoned me.

Bright as jewels in a bride's ear,
all my men went away."

2

The young Kurdish militiaman teaching me to use
the RPG says if it sees
an armored vehicle speeding toward us

it wants to aim low, but if the enemy's dug in
to a mountain, then it wants to aim
high so shrapnel rains down.

Now the RPG balanced on my shoulder
moves one leg forward, one back,
focusing my eye through the scope's crosshairs

zeroing in on a line of burnt-out tanks. It tells me
to trust its trigger under my finger
secure under his finger as he

screws the booster into the warhead, his breath
and mine fusing with its smell of sulfur,
metallic sweat, its barrel smooth

against my cheek, its body through
his body pressing so close to mine
you can't tell who is who, nor do you

want to—finger over finger
pulls the trigger, marrying our eye
to its trajectory low and flat through air

rippling with the whoosh of flame
above weeds recoiling, fins spinning
counter to the wind as our threesome

embraces in the heat emanating
off armor plate, the always-approaching
moment of penetration exploding

in a far-off puff of smoke and heat.
"Now you are one of us," he smiles and taps
my helmet. And almost apologetic,

"But my dearest friend, if they spot
our position after we shoot, you must please
remember to please hit the dirt or we'll get shot."

3

At the opening he asks me for
a cigarette, then says, "She could be my sister."
In her picture before us, dressed up for

a party, sipping tea, she stares past me
to meet her own eyes in another picture
where, in uniform, she holds an RPG,

face calm, unsmiling, the caption claiming
she was blown up by a bomb. But in the next
picture he tells me she shot down

the helicopter wobbling, the pilot
in the cockpit a thumb-smear of smoke above
the room loud with laughter and chitchat.

4

The poet who wrote "Competence with pain, /
. . . a bite and sup, / We hug our little destiny again,"
what would he say to her, to the orange flame

that was the pilot? Where would he stand to see
what they could see? But the bomb that blots
out the sky in the cockpit blank as the eye

of a dragonfly knows nothing of itself
or the nothing it turns into or the nothing
grasping nothing it also knows nothing of.

Homage to Vallejo's
"Hymn to the Volunteers of the Republic"

Another Disgrace

I don't know what to do or where to stand:
I write, I break things, I clap my hands, I rush around,
I cry out, I put out fires, I tell my heart, It's over.
I say to all the bones of marching soldiers

in their worldwide exhaustion, Don't volunteer!
Sure, I'm a disgrace, but my forehead's impersonal—
it's the architect of my most famous fall
which the animal part of me most honors.

Its instincts are the ropes I climb
into smoke that swirls above my gravestone—
me, just another four-legged human

unable to hold in my paws ecstatic time
where my black-tie pettiness collides
against each second's double-edged speed.

Twilight in the Future

Gunpowder bites at its own elbows.
I clench the bit in my good American teeth.
The nativities of dictators, the shows
of grief from bacteria nuked to death

are recorded by atmospheric needles
raising data to the nth power of martyrdom.
If you think about Goya as he kneels
in prayer before a mirror, or the Cartesian

attack on the straight line leading to the clouds,
or Quevedo's wit exploding like dynamite,
or Cajal devoured by his own microscopic slides,

or Teresa dying because she does not die,
then every child-soldier of the absent proletariat
climbs a sputtering flame into the sky.

Dream Dreamed a Millennium Too Late

I dreamed that I was good. I dreamed it
when I lay down at the foot, not of my bed,
but of my own illiterate forehead. I dreamed it
for the ashes lining the dead roads,

I dreamed it for the murderers as much
as for the murdered. I dreamed it for the genius
wandering barefoot with his flocks, for the smooth
and for the rough, for all the hidden voices

spreading rumors about death dying.
I dreamed that I was good in a bygone
age of camels. And yet the dinosaurs keep on dying,

they follow two steps behind me, while one
step away the flood rushes toward the horizon
to see its own limits before the ocean burns.

What I Can Say in 2021 about a Famine in 2011

I said after watching a goat climb into a huge cooking pot and lick it clean, *The war is over*—but the goat said, *Another one is starting*—

I said after he said that he kept his trousers rolled to keep his cuffs from touching dirt, *The city is divided green zone red zone but there's nothing red or green about it.*

I said, *I'm dead. Good riddance, fuckhead,* half-joking.

I said, and half meant it, *I threw off death, I put my bones back together.*

I said, *Rembrandt painting Moses smashing the tablets of the Law channels the nearsighted wrath of a bony billy goat lunging on his rope.*

I said, *I tangle my horns in a thicket.*

I said what Mrs. Nfumi said the day we saw a tiny one-room schoolhouse afloat in a flooding creek, *This is what happens when hunger is what is.*

I said, *The way that kid held out his hand to me, forefingers and thumb pinched together, calling out, "American American . . ."*

I said, *It's your turn to wait night after night like the boy sitting in his plastic chair as all the other kids gather under the tent.*

I said what Isaac didn't say, *There's no father with a knife to cut my throat.*

I said, *There's this other kid who said how he and his friends like to play cards and since there aren't any cards the cards are invisible and they slap them down hard, arguing, laughing, on high alert all afternoon for the card that breaks the game until it's time to stop playing and get your rations.*

I said what one Kenyan soldier said, *Why wouldn't Adam in the Garden hide from God if all God was doing was checking to see if Adam had fucked up?*

I said, *Jab me with a needle and squirt an eyedropper of vitamins down my throat.*

I said, *I woke to a spider crawling across my wrist.*

I said, *Here they come from the Grease Pit Bar, an embassy of ghosts who never again will have to turn the other cheek.*

Clearance

For sale: two tours of duty in Afghanistan of the sniper
turned musher to mutts pulling a dogsled
at Snowmass. The animal in him touched by
the essence of animal
                              staining the snow yellow,
his scopes hidden under his cot in the bunkhouse.

For sale: continent under continent, the ocean shelving down,
the blood of a whale pouring out of the gate
of a flatbed truck
                              and pattering like soft rain on the tarmac.
A chainsaw hacks through blubber but stops short
of the vertebrae set end to end like whiskey kegs.

For sale: ghosts lining up like girders
made of COR-TEN steel, the air ionized by their ectoplasmic flesh
so that the hair inside your nostrils
                              turns electric when they pass.

Scraps of voices, clanging resurrections, rusted hymns sung
by deactivated RPGs, creaking hosannas
of army surplus warehouses,
                              bargain-basement prices
for the military slang of the Second Ass Crack Regiment
putting in for leave time at Fort Fumble.

For sale: the otherworldly sergeant lifting weights
like an old-time strongman,
                              a thick leather belt cinching
his waist as if his strength—or weakness?—
                                        could barely be contained.

For sale: your self inside the blast wave
shattering the show window, its vacuum sucking all the suits
into the street: scorched linen sleeve
                                        of a forty-four-long
ready-to-wear for weddings, funerals, christenings.

For sale: all voids, all empty spaces, all time
torn off unused between what people say
are life's greatest events
                                        and the unnoticed quiet
of water polishing stone, wearing ever smoother
each atom always moving.

Last Cigarette

After the explosions, the big one of the big bang,
the little one of the firecrackers set by some kid

off in weeds in the field, not a sound in outer space
or here back on Earth disturbs the perfect peace

of the unmoving afternoon. The body of the soldier
I saw lying asleep in his hut of scrap metal on top of a hill,

or the stop-time photo of the meteor slamming
into the atmosphere, float in the clear air, forever

part of a moment that in a moment will disappear.
Today is a long day in which death keeps coming closer,

but still elsewhere, off in the electronic ether,
though the soldier could be dead, his last image

of himself exploding through the air through the minefield
he walked in among the orange trees, unaware

of the grenade that caught him smoking in the shade.
Flicking with his thumb his lighter's flint striker,

not worrying at that moment about living forever,
the field he's walking in through this stillness

without end is an island drifting through the void.

Apology to My Daughter

Life is not a walk across a field.
—BORIS PASTERNAK

For ten years, Hannah, the world convinced me
that thorn trees, desert, Land Rovers tricked out
with CB radios, machine guns and armor plate,

grew more real the harder it became
to fulfill my nightly promise to rebar and rubble
that some final vowel would reverse time

and resurrect stunted concrete into a city.
Stretched to the horizon, a smoking, vacant lot;
overgrown weeds and vines; a real nightingale

flitting among leaves. I didn't know it
back then, but when I left you, Hannah, I suspected
private life, underneath, was pure evasion.

But I learned there's no shortage of suffering—
that a father's no shield for his child
when life is, in fact, a walk across a field.

III

Breaker

There Sarah and I are, all those years ago, and Hannah, still just a little girl, too scared, defiant, jealous to leave her mother for long as she took her very first walk with me down the beach that afternoon. The waves, running white against the offshore wind, sent up spray blowing off the wave-tops as they shaped into green tents where a seal, magnified in its glide down the foaming face, mirrored her bundled energy and grace as she refused to take my hand, reminding me how different she was, is, from me when I was a child—so malleable to my parents' moods, an inward sulk I never showed my only rebellion. Wind blew salt in both our faces which she licked off her lips—"Come on, Hannah," I said, "let's keep walking," but suddenly she turned from me and ran toward Sarah, running the way a foal does, all instinct and anxious need, toward its mother.

And now all those years ago are swept away at an outdoor restaurant, the sun cool but bright, and she's happy to see us, she rolls her eyes at my jokes which is why I tell them, knowing that if she mocks me she still trusts me, her compass needle swiveling this way, that, but always pointing out beyond us who once were her circumference now shrinking to so much less.

Breaker on breaker other lives pour over hers, as right now on the phone, a friend's voice, brave but gnawed at by rage and fear, tells me about her brain tumor, how she can't make her eyes focus, how she can't find herself in space, how the attendants at the rehab place won't let her go to the bathroom by herself because she'll fall, but then she asks what's up with Hannah, how's Hannah . . .

Youth, age. Sitting here alone, staring at the cement water tower on top of the old brick housing complex, the leaves on the plane trees faintly turning yellow, shuffling in the light breeze, how do all these hours enter into one life that keeps telling me, none too convincingly, that it's mine? It's as if I'm that seal tented in the wave, my path down the breaker a slow-motion glide that seems never to end . . . but how short a span until the wave heels over and crumples around me, exploding every which way in foam and spray as I pop up above the waves, curious and wary of what the humans are doing, the little one turning from the big one and running away.

Ostrich

Your face turns to smoke again and again
behind the tinted window

of our generation that dies with such precision
it's ludicrous to mourn us, itchy arguers

who aspired to have a conscience:
you're dead, I know, but I still talk to you,

hand cupped to your ear, talking the world
into a corner, loving the fragility

of forgiving yourself what your enemies—and sometimes
your friends—couldn't forgive. Some called you out,

some called you the last ostrich
of honesty. Your long dying

is finally dead, I know, but I still talk to you—
the distance our anti-intimacy must still cross.

I knew you well enough to be afraid of you
and love you, to know your elsewhere is my only here,

to long to hear your fingers typing in the ether
one of your barbwire letters

that every time I read cuts into my palms.
You put your hand on the glass,

I put my hand over yours, palm to palm not touching—
unless heat radiating through glass is a kind of touching.

At Yeats's Tower

My wife surprised me by attempting automatic writing. . . . I . . . offered to spend what remained of life explaining and piecing together those scattered sentences. 'No,' was the answer, 'we have come to give you metaphors for poetry.'
—W. B. YEATS, *A VISION*

Climbing and climbing the winding stair
I saw my father coming down from the tower,
dead now twenty years, his goatee gone white
blending with his collar. His raw folly
in coming back to give me metaphors
for poetry left me wondering
about such otherworldly faith in a man who,
when I asked him if he believed in anything
after we were dead, simply wrinkled up
his nose and said, "No, why would there be?"
At that moment I wanted somehow to save
him from fading completely out of memory—
but as he passed me on the stair he said
nothing, and for all I know, nothing was what
he saw as he went by and kept descending.

Descending to where? To the parking lot
at the bottom of the tower? Down a stairway the living
can't see, a stairway that makes its way down
under the streambed and the cow drinking
in its own reflection? White shirt, brown jacket,
dark brown slacks, he seemed enclosed in his
habitual isolation, tucking a meaning
into a glance that bears no explanation,
his half-seen face behind his newspaper making
him unreachable, his shyness and gentleness
and stillness as thickly walled-in as these
humid stone stairs weeping in the cracks.

Instead of painful and by now useless reckonings,
I would have pointed out to him a letter
in a vitrine like the relic of a martyr, Yeats's
slashing handwriting insisting to the estate agent
that the spring flood and damp make the winding stair
slippery, the stones chilly if not tubercular,
so would a hundred-pound reduction in price
not be in order? My father would have understood
about the money, having joined the Paupers Investment Club
(aptly named, my mother said), which invested in
a scheme that could make played-out gold mines
profitable again by molecular extraction
of gold from tailings, like Rumpelstiltskin
spinning straw into gold. The CEO absconded
with the Paupers' money and my father,
for him at least, lost big time. I can see my father
studying on the brochure the confident face
that he now knew was nothing but a mask—
though Yeats would have insisted that all of us
wear masks, so wouldn't it be better to choose
the mask you wear? And since the choice is yours,
why not choose the mask the very opposite of all
you fear you are? As if the CEO, wanting to be
bold but suspecting he was timid, so persisted
in his mask it became his face which, despite
his crime, at least had the virtue of being legible.

My father would never have said so, but he would
have thought this was silly, consistent
with Yeats's whispered nickname, Silly Willie:
anyone who wore a mask was out to fool
the world as my father had been fooled, so what
did it matter if it was mask or face smiling
its pixilated smile from a brochure?
And if my father were to steal Yeats's metaphors,

he might have said that the rough beast in our
faces, slouching to die in each other's eyes,
knows nothing of masks—that in its teeth and fur
it's all the face there is because, Silly Willie,
isn't it true that no matter how long you
wear them, masks don't grieve, only faces do?

Queen for a Day

The white dog on the deck next door looks exhausted. He glances up from time to time when a distant jackhammer, a nail gun wakes him from his dozing.

I and the white dog commune together, how he lost a front leg to cancer: a vet, anesthesia, money. The dog may not know about money, but he knows the bone saw and the hand that held it.

Maybe I'm the dog's orphaned leg. I hop around looking for a creature like the dog, but when he sees me, smells me, he doesn't know me anymore. His limp is no limp just the way he walks and runs, maimed but perfectly OK with it, not needing anything other than his three-leggedness.

Or maybe the white dog is a kind of prayer, the way Jesus was the kind of son who keeps pushing the boulder out of his way as he steps forth from the cave on the third day. And there I am, Thomas putting my finger in his wounds.

Now, the white dog studies sunlight shifting, the deck's grain swirling, his eyes lost in a self-forgetful reverie that one moment watches the hatch of flies rising past the black railings, then slide into sleep.

But what if I could speak? Speak my hacked-off misery, sadness, loss as on the old TV show, the studio audience applauding dead husband, child sick with cancer, each misfortune vying with the other to shoot the applause meter to the top? How would *you* like to be Queen for a Day? The ermine stole wraps around sobbing shoulders, the jeweled crown rests heavy on the brow, the winner who's also the loser sits on the red-velvet throne and listens to the grave, sonorous male voice unveiling the list of prizes: new washing machine, vacation to Hawaii, brand-new cake mixer, flower-embroidered smock and apron, an envelope of cash.

The white dog just keeps on dozing, waking . . . now he rouses, limps a few steps and barks at the flies rising on the thermals carrying them up higher where swallows eat them as if all this swooping, so wondrous to observe, can't be stopped.

Stethoscope

The Unified Field

It wasn't that there was anything to say
that would stop him from feeling this way—the X
of himself splayed out in space

where gravity was weakest. He and his father
and his talkative mother
suffering tiny little strokes that took away

this syllable from this word, that syllable
from that, all this lay
in one pan of the balance scale

while in the other there was nothing but dark matter
and the cosmic inconsequence
of his literal physical heart beating.

And then the unified field, faced with its own emptiness,
bent down to his chest as if to listen.

A Toast to Pavlov's Dogs

Oh Leash held by a hand I can't see, here
in the laboratory where nothing can change
and where yips and bites are fine-tuned to the pack's mentality,

am I one of his dogs, the three-legged one that knows nothing
of my lack except for how I bark, growl,
and whine to be let in? Am I the salivating triangle

guided only by my nose that keeps me
on the move in my limping trot away from you, Leash, yanking
me back from all the filth I want to shove my nose in?

Why won't you let me go free? The sad gestures
of our growing intimacy is a reflex we
can't escape or express: sometimes, emotion is just mange.

So Leash, here's a toast to my lab pals: August, Fast One,
Pretty Little Lady, Joy, Beauty, Milord, Clown.

The Judgment after the Last

What would we like to see happen?
Would we like to drive nails into our hands?
Would the shame engulfing us like flame

on a computer screen make us understand
that throwing a match into the Grand Canyon
while snapping a selfie, and never once thinking

how far that match falls, is the original sin
that a donkey's ears, twitching
as we ride to the bottom, reveal as the truth

about our consciences? How many nails
will we need? Go to the movies, do research,
be the Regulator forced to kill kill kill

and that's when we'll find out just who we are
or if there's anything like "who" anymore.

Mission

It's not simply that the palm trees are on fire
but that they waver up more fire than fire,
brighter and harsher and more intoxicating

than the flames spreading ever thought of being—
the thick black smoke turning noon to midnight
rears up in a wall that nobody can see

over or around or through even as this nobody
comes crashing through the screen
right into my living room: poor nobody! In this loneliest of times,

he tells me how much he loves me, how his lack
and mine feel somehow the same and that the flames
crawling over him have become his mission:

burning, he erects a burning house of smoke
we can neither live in or abandon.

Sunday Is Never the Last Day of the Week

Using zip ties and velcro to strap on a homemade bomb,
who is to blame, who should have told us that on the far side
of the screen in this Sunday calm our generation has had its time?

In that corner where we slept together
so many nights, yes, in that corner where the bed
of our democratic hour has been put out with all the other

Monday morning trash, there are always two doors
opening and closing as one of us goes out and the other
comes in. Why couldn't we show our love for one another

the way the void dissolves into the zero? Why did the animal
grafted to the human find such satisfaction in explosions?
Darkness to darkness, ashes to ashes, the animal to the human,

why shouldn't we take pleasure where and when we can—
provided this is pleasure, provided that the body isn't null.

Last Rites

Even if the suit they dress me in for my funeral
is dry-cleaned at Perfection Laundry, then washed
and washed in the blood of the lamb, the knees

will still be muddy from kneeling down, the sleeves,
mismatched, will tell their own threadbare tale
about the breath of life breathed into tabletop dust.

What would the naked man and woman and talking snake say
about the god who no longer remembers if they're forgiven
or not? Listening as a kid to the old stories,

there were never enough beanstalks and giants
and Jacks. Now, the pallbearers pick up my coffin,
they carry me out to the ruined cathedral where the saints'

wooden faces, frozen in their homely expressions of grace,
are shadowed by flocks of blackbirds whirling past.

The Hunger Artist as a Senior Citizen

Nowadays, in my cage
in old straw, where
my brother-keeper

forgets to come feed me anymore,
at last I'm fasting for its own sake,
not to break records I've broken

a thousand times before.
Besides, nothing could be easier
than to starve forever

if the food they keep on
giving you makes you sick.
This hunger is a moment's

vision that will persist
in a pillar of radiant house dust.

A Man Plays Debussy for a Blind, Eighty-Four-Year-Old Female Elephant

I read today how when a poet was going mad,
hearing voices under his bed, his friend hid
a speaking tube inside the wall and would whisper
"encouraging suggestions" that the poet
shouldn't kill himself—should wait till after
breakfast when sun and sausages and eggs
would put him in a more hopeful frame of mind.
But my friend Liam killed himself, and Tree,
his wife, said that was what he wanted:
nobody should pity her or him, which, by the same token,
reminds me of the young Palestinian woman
at a protest telling me just after she was tear-gassed
how she had "no regrets," my voice coming
out of nowhere since her eyes, stinging,
were tearing up so badly she couldn't see.

And yet today when I read how a poet was going mad,
hearing voices, there was another voice
inside me interfering with the voice that said,
"You're better off dead, you useless piece of shit"—
only it wasn't a voice but a melody echoing
from an out-of-tune piano that a man
alone in the bush was playing for an elephant—
an old blind female in her baggy hide
and cataracted eyes who had spent her life
hauling logs, being beaten and abused, and now kept
her distance from the herd, a loner, restless,
or so her keepers at Elephants World said—
but listening to the music seemed to calm her,
her homely flat feet shuffling side to side,

her ears flapping to cool herself but also to show pleasure,
even joy, yeah, that's what they claimed, joy—
as the quiet melancholy rising to near ecstasy
of "Clair de lune" ascends to the high notes
where elephant and pianist and listener
all meld before "descending gradually
to more lush and subtly darker harmonies."

Today I read how a poet going mad—
but you've heard all that before—when I
was a boy all we kids played elephant,
swinging our arms like trunks as we shuffled
head to tail or stampeded across the playground
driving off the lions and tigers and trampling
our science teacher, Mr. Allen, his little glasses
flying off his head as we joyously stomped him,
trumpeting aloud! Why did we so hate him?
And why can't I stop seeing that greenish pall
of tear gas hanging heavy above the street?
It's as if invisible fingers keep playing on our neurons
as man and elephant walk off into the bush
and just before the underbrush closes in
both come to a halt and stand facing one another,
the man patting her trunk curling around him
to rest on his shoulder as he shuts his eyes and leans
his forehead against hers; it's like each one's
listening to what the other's thinking, elephant thoughts
of chains and things to eat, human ones
of poets, sane or mad, until the music goes still
and both elephant and human dissolve into sunlight
falling on the piano all alone among the hills.

My Mother as the Eyes of a Whale
on Her Ninety-Second Birthday

Ripples wracked to chop inside the harbor,
swell blown back to whitewater,

deep ocean drawing a dark line, the whale turns
emerald passing under the stern,

pupils tiny in the huge maul head, eyes
the size of a colt's eyes, but located like

its ears on either side of the head so that the pupils can't
see what's coming from behind, nor what's

swimming toward it from the future—
as if the salt-and-pepper head were

to tower upward like a great mountain
between two lakes in the valley so that your pained

eyes would always see two different sights
at the same time—in one eye, your sleepless nights,

in the other, your drifting, lightless zones.

Conversation

When David asks, "Where does the saying 'She still has
her marbles' come from?" I'd been talking about my ma,
who's 94, same as David, though David said,
"I'm 94 and four months, so she's still a child."
I say, "It's got to come from being a kid, wouldn't you think,
and playing marbles?" "Yes," he says, "it probably must.
But Tom, do kids even play marbles anymore?"
Earlier, he'd said, "I live in a place called Brook Haven,
but we all call it The Death Camp. There are some nice people
who live in The Death Camp, people I've known a long time
who have a sense of humor, or try to have one,
about their situation, but the problem is the horizon
is foreshortened, if you know what I mean . . ."
Then David says, "You know there's that poem about
the two shepherds who sing verses out of Virgil
and the moment one of them finishes, the other says,
'That's just fantastic, it's wonderful!' and the shepherds
seem like they love one another because the other one
starts singing different lines of Virgil and when
he finishes his friend says, 'That's just fantastic,
it's wonderful!' and of course, it's Virgil pulling
all the strings, the shepherds are Virgil acting like
shepherds who are quoting Virgil whom they love.
I saw Arthur's widow, Marie-Claire, to show her
a book in which Arthur's and my poems had been translated
into French and she was gracious and enthusiastic
as always, but then she asked me if I'd ever been
to visit her in this apartment where I'd been
to see them lots, so even though she wasn't sure
of exactly who I was, at least she knew enough to know
that I was somebody she was supposed to be fond of—
but by how she kept smiling at me, she was anxious

for us both to act like she knew me."

"So she sort of knew who
you were," I said. But David, who has no truck with
the pathos of old age even as he feels it, didn't answer.

Outside my window were seagulls coasting and being
buffeted above the whitecaps in a bright glare
that was hard to stare into. We were coming to the end
of what we were saying, and now obligatory emotions
which we nonetheless honored gave our saying
goodbye an artificial quality, a forced
heartiness of affection until David quoted
from a poem, not his, referring to the Sphinx's beard,
"It's in the cellar of the British Museum
where the Athenians lost their marbles,"
and then David said, "Much love," and we were
off the phone and I stored his number
in my Contacts and erased the two 617
numbers for the 857 number and wondered
what he'd say if he knew that someone had made
a virtual-reality app of Bergen-Belsen
and that the next step is to make it "more tailored
and personalized for visitors."

One other thing David said:
"All my new poems ask questions like, 'Who is this who
who is saying this and what, anyway, is the this?'"

For My Mother's Ninety-Sixth Birthday

The pack ice underneath me was beginning
to break up. I was isolated on a floe
and every now and then a killer whale
would jut up from the water
with its little pig eyes,
its great blunt socket teeth glinting through frost smoke
hanging above the current tugging me
out to sea
where packs of killer whales raced up and down
the leads like racehorses.

Where I was going wasn't clear, didn't need to be.
I felt snow brush by my cheek
like my mother's makeup brush—
and staring back at me,
disembodied in the mirror, her plucked eyebrows
floated high above her gaze reflected back.

Nothing I could do could make her eyes
not turn to ice. Everywhere there was famine, cold,
and complete stillness. But then I heard far-off
salsa blasting from a car window,
a trumpet playing a syncopated figure above high C
just like the one I loved to practice
when I was fifteen, a little *dut-a-lut-dut* I usually clammed—
but when I hit the notes right the frost smoke
lifted and you could see from Mt. Erebus halfway across the world.

The music crawled away, echoing down the street.
The killer whales kept leaning against my ice floe.
My mother and the killer whale locked eyes.

It was over then, this little vision of our future,
paranoid maybe, but oddly splendid.

Out on the open sea, stranded on the ice, the fine muscles
of someone's embouchure was playing the impossible
while my mother and I, beyond help, listened to it, in love with it.

IV

The King's Touch
after an MRI

Up through shifting blues
to where the sun is coolly ignorant
of where I lie on the sea bottom
lit by my own storm-light flickering,

I hear the tech's voice wrapped in space-dark
scuttling through black light,
Please don't move, Mr. Sleigh.
All around me the room is stammering,

iron smashing against iron,
a robot drummer pounding out
the earth's magnetic field
slicing my brain into a geode's

crystalline amethyst.
Lying in my underwear, T-shirt,
and holey socks, my head wedged
to keep it still, I feel

coming closer the king's hand—
poor squeamish
king, cursed by the power
to cure, having to touch

all us sufferers
with our ugly, swollen glands.
But why shouldn't
the king's touch cure me?

Caught like an astronaut
against the ocean's curve
lit by the sun rising,
I can see the tech back on earth

reflected in the metal halo
hovering above my skull.
Spinning crazily as dials
on an old dynamo,

my body's
beyond control, outside of me
staring up at my own
neuter attachments.

In front of me the whole earth
shines in its neural blaze.
And the tumor in my brain
goes on its own space walk,

free to drift where gravity
takes it, my tumor
that like a mother
talks to me in dreams, asking,

Tom, do you have your suitcase?
Did you remember
your razor and your toothbrush?
Have you packed your shoes?

Little Testament

1

No drip line to uncrimp, no one needing
to intubate the moon or hold the little plastic basin
to the sky's lips. "The sun is an insult," wrote one.

Millions on millions of stacked-up rooms
where screens become a hive mind
thinking it, seeing it, saying it over and over again.

We didn't not choose this, but go on attending
to the gardener and his pruning knife
"busy about the tree of life"

uprooted by the screen's virtual distress.
Only the microbe is natural. And all the rest,
is that just looking for solace in the magnolia's feverish

pink flesh while I wait for one of us to come down sick,
our breath turning raggedy, historic?

2

The sun comes up and goes on insulting me.

The East River keeps on flowing out to sea.

Sea snow keeps falling, feathers, bits of bone,

as yet undevoured pieces of flesh drifting down,

always down through these inky slicks of oil.

—This is for real, y'all, This is for real,

Oh Lord, please have mercy, the man keeps yelling

into his phone, craning his neck

to get a glimpse of a forklift lifting

body bags into a refrigerator truck.

But even as I listen, wanting to protect you

from the river's quiet rant,

a pair of plastic gloves eddies in the current,

the fingers sluicing what comes through.

3

You want to say every room
is an emergency room.
You want to say

every room is packed
with voices
like the old movie

when a woman locks
herself inside her room
and tries

to keep from going crazy
from all the faces
pushing through the walls.

But to want to say
isn't what it
is for us, it's just me

texting you on
the far side of
the wall

where I
keep mistaking your cough
for a laugh.

4

The old men on the corner who play dominoes
have been dispersed
but their radio's ghost

reverberates under the tree
they hung with their kids'
worn-out toys,

Mickey and Minnie
swaying to "Qué Buena"
in *La Catedral de la Salsa*

drifting and perishing
above us in the air at the wedding
between my lack of clarity

and these jails of light in the sky
where I keep on stupidly insisting we'll never die.

5

Everybody has put on their mask
that looks just like their face only the face
lets you know it's just a mask.

I don't know how to solve this
or make it less frightening
that spring leafing out

seems somehow to be agreeing
with the guy on the radio
who's sobbing, really sobbing,

sick himself as he worries
about his sick wife
and his still-well son,

that if he should die
what difference would it make, and why?

6

I was dead. The hospital around me
pinged and beeped, and though I lay
on my bed, the nurses and doctors couldn't

see me. I kept saying to myself, Why doesn't
somebody come? And then the feeling changed,
and I was climbing and climbing crumbling stairs,

breathing hard but enjoying it, the moss between
the brick slick and such a deep green
that I knew I was a boy again.

My dead father waited for me at the top
where he lay coiled round and round himself
just like the little green garden snake

we found frozen one morning on the front step
during a late spring cold snap.
He'd been trying to shed his skin

but somehow he'd gotten stuck partway in
and out of his old body. He looked perplexed,
his tongue tasting the air, flicking

across his thin snake lips, listening
through his tiny snake ears to my breath
coming closer, his eyes seeming disappointed

as if it were my fault that he hadn't gotten farther.
I picked him up, he writhed up my arm
and coiled around my neck and lay

quiet, waiting, cold against my shoulder.

7

In Rilke's poem about washing a dead body
one of the women doing the washing stops
to cough, and as she coughs she leaves the heavy
sponge of vinegar on the corpse's face.

What Rilke called the horrible and apparently
repulsive is also what is with everything
else that is. My daughter tells me that her therapist
tells her that the therapist's brother, a rich doctor,

bought himself his own private ventilator on eBay:
$30K. How automatic to judge him, to dismiss
his fear. But when the Callery pear's
white blossoms start to scatter, and I read how flowers

also feel fear, there the doctor is in the everything
that is. "Beauty is the quality of perfect continuity."
"Grub first, then ethics." Would the sponge of vinegar
on the doctor's face while his hand, cramped,

tries to demonstrate how he no longer thirsts,
give him the smell of cooked spinach?
In my own little dance with death,
my shadow's been lying on the blank page

for a while, and Death, his fingers trembling
with pleasure, reaches from behind to take
my hand cramping up around the pencil,
intending to write my last word himself.

8

Telling you my dream over Zoom, your screen
freezes, your face shatters into snow
as we wait for you to finish quarantine.

I sprayed disinfectant on a cartoon devil
but it was really holy water that sizzled
when it scorched the devil's flesh.

Poor old devil, you laugh, rubbing
thumb and forefingers together
in that way that says to strays (including devils),

Don't worry, I'm your friend, now roll
over and let me scratch your belly,
that's right, that's right, aren't you a beauty?

9

The sun soars
then creeps
down to the river

where we walk
its banks on
the lookout

for our sickness
jogging toward
us, spit flying

from our
mouths, trigger
bars locked

down. Vectors
scattering the rhetoric
and numbers,

we stand
away from the others
on the subway platform

sharing our generation's
little testament
to dying

until the train
doors open
and we step in

to this lurching anti-heaven
carrying us
to Hoyt-Schermerhorn.

10

This isn't the season of phantasmal peace, no bird nation
lifts the earth in a net of shadows, but still the birds have taken

the city back: on the fire escape doves sidestep past us,
not noticing our shadows falling on the glass.

Some I love have become the shadow of "the waxwing slain /
By the false azure in the windowpane"

as the water tower's shadow rises above a delivery truck
where a take-out menu kites like a hawk.

In poor exhausted Psyche's garage underground,
months will go by before the all clear sounds—

but until then we can watch their silhouettes
ruffling across the blinds, keeping separate,

headstrong heads moving in syncopated ardor
before they groom each other's gray sleek feathers.

The King's Evil

I'm trying not to be bored so I watch a poem capsize in front of me. It tells me all suffering is worthy, redeemable by the sound of a rowboat passing between one Greek island and another in the dead of night.

But the rowboat keeps getting lost in mist, the oarsman shouts, *Where am I?* but all he hears are oars splashing.

But what if there's a demon chasing the boat, would the demon's wet eyes tell another story about the poem now drowning in waves of secret and violent inhumanity, waves pouring over all this sentimentality?

I want to see the demon swimming an Olympic-gold-medal-Michael Phelps crawl, to see if he's being ridden by a monkey in the faded slang of the 1950s the way Phelps was in victory.

Failure or gold, who doesn't want to feel that their body is theirs, that no sickness of soul or body can steal that?

The King's hand reaches out to heal my neck wearing the frilled ulcerated ruff, the weeping wounds of the King's Evil.

Bless the rowboat, the oarsman, the Greek islands, bless the wound, the King's Touch that exposes aversion to experience, fear of life, an arid heart.

But most of all, bless the demon who grabs the keel and climbs into the boat and squats on the poet's hands so he can't type or write or reach out his hands to touch or be touched, to heal or hurt.

The King's Evil and the King's Touch are two faces of the King who, when He touches the open raw sores of TB germs inflaming the lymph nodes and ulcerating the skin of His subjects, wonders for a moment if He isn't a demon like the demons in His book that He wants to banish from His kingdom, but they're everywhere you look and the more you look the more you find them, which is why the King's Evil needs us, loves us, and wants us to be healed so it can prove to the King just how sick His subjects are, though spirits worth saving if the saving can be done in a way that doesn't lead to demons entering our skin.

Oh King, I pray, don't let me die today, in such and such a way, let me feel Your sanctified Touch which is only a human being's that God, like a hand slipping inside a plastic surgical glove, is using for whatever blessing the demon swimming after the boat wants to stop.

Have mercy on us today, and if not today, tomorrow, and if not tomorrow, the day after, and so forth.

Age of Wonder

It was our age of wonder; and then it was over.
Somehow we'd survived: Now, what else

would be expected of us? On the shelf
the scavenged glass bottles polished

by the waves, the dregs of medicines and tinctures
that cured nobody of anything

but the pain of suspecting nothing
could alleviate their pain; that blue that spangled

up the wall across the ceiling
and which we woke to clear mornings, shadows

of locust trees playing over the covers,
that was the moment the empty bottles spilled over:

What did I think wonder meant until I met you?
And the fact that it could go on and on?

My age of wonder assaults me in the mirror:
Is this still me lying next to you?

Even our peeling wallpaper, finely crosshatched
and crinkling like the skin thinning

on the back of my hand, is charged
with that blue shattering into prisms

faint all across the wall—but it's no rainbow,
that isn't the wonder that either of us

craved, the rays vibrating
never threw open glitzy, sunset-colored doors

to some personal heaven we could
or couldn't enter. Instead, one or the other of us

finally came down from the attic, ready to smell
the rich, mudflat dolor

of low tide, the subtle sulfurous rot
of dead gulls, gutted fish, bleaching salt hay.

And as for the age, the wonder is that the age
lasted this long. And now that it's over,

we can still live, can't we, inside its fading, as if it were the future
that year by year we age backward toward?

Notes

"Confession" adapts the line "the sea has soaked your heart through" from George Chapman's version of Homer's *The Odyssey*, Book V. I came across the line in Adam Nicolson's *Why Homer Matters*, page 25.

"Dead Me, Live Me" is in part based on a passage in Robert Macfarlane's *Underland*.

In "Reading," in section 1, the novel *Petals of Blood* is by Ngũgĩ wa Thiong'o. In section 3, I quote from *The Narrative of the Life of Frederick Douglass*, and from *The Interesting Narrative of the Life of Olaudah Equiano*. The details of a founding father who was considering selling a slave to buy books (James Madison eventually decided not to sell William Gardner as a slave, but he bound him as an indentured servant) is taken from Jill Lepore's *These Truths: A History of the United States*. Section 4 is taken from "A South African Poet on His Imprisonment," an article about Breyten Breytenbach, published by Donald Woods in the *New York Times*. Section 5 is based on a letter by Macchiavelli sent to me by Michael Collier. It also incorporates a phrase from Ernest Hemingway's *A Moveable Feast*. Section 6 is based on John Hersey's article for the *New Yorker*, "Hiroshima," as well as an episode from the TV show *The Twilight Zone*.

"Words from Chernobyl" is based on Svetlana Alexievich's *Voices from Chernobyl: The Oral History of a Nuclear Disaster*.

In "Practice Range," the jihadist poems are taken from various online sources such as the *Atlantic* article by Joanna Paraszczuk entitled "The Poems of Jihadists."

"Ostrich" is for Tony Hoagland. The final lines are based on a dream David Rivard told me.

In "Stethoscope," in the last section, "The Hunger Artist as a Senior Citizen," I take the title from Franz Kafka's short story "The Hunger Artist."

"My Mother as the Eyes of a Whale on Her Ninety-Second Birthday" is based on a passage in *Moby-Dick*.

"The King's Touch" refers to the traditional belief that the king, as God's divine representative, can lay hands on the sick and heal them. The king I have in mind, and whose portrait is on the cover, is King James VI of Scotland—though later, when he ruled over both Scotland and England, he was called James I. Although he believed himself to be deeply devout, he was also said to be deeply squeamish about touching all those proffered ulcers and wounds. Like most of Europe in his day (1566–1625), James believed in witchcraft, magic, and sorcery, and wrote a book, *Daemonologie*, which attempts to prove that such forces exist, and which also describes the gruesome tortures and punishments he presided over in the North Berwick witch trials. For me, the contradiction between James's divine pretentions and his use of torture, as well as the personal revulsion he felt for the rite of laying on of hands, suggest how mystery, power, and the secular collide.

In "Little Testament," section 1 uses a phrase from Robert Lowell's "Waking Early Sunday Morning." Section 10 incorporates the title of Derek Walcott's poem "The Season of Phantasmal Peace," as well as the first two lines of Vladimir Nabokov's poem "Pale Fire."

"The King's Evil" incorporates phrases from a James Baldwin quote about sentimentality that appears in his essay "Everybody's Protest Novel":

> *Sentimentality, the ostentatious parading of excessive and spurious emotion, is the mark of dishonesty, the inability to feel; the wet eyes of the sentimentalist betray his aversion to experience, his fear of life, his arid heart; and it is always, therefore, the signal of secret and violent inhumanity, the mask of cruelty.*

In addition, "The King's Evil" is a traditional name for scrofula, a form of tubercular infection that inflames the lymph nodes so that they become swollen, and can create ulcerative lesions. Because it was one of the most prevalent diseases that King James I was required to cure by a laying on of hands (see note above on "The King's Touch"), it came to be known as the King's Evil. Given James's penchant for torture in pursuit of witches, the King's Evil could well refer to the demonic side of the King's own nature—not least because of his paranoid embrace of conspiracy theories. James wrote in his treatise on witchcraft, *Daemonologie*, how he had heard rumors of witches conspiring against him on his voyage from Scotland to Denmark to bring back his new bride,

Anne—rumors which he had then found to be true. He recounts how these witches had christened a cat, tied to said cat "the cheefest parts of a dead man, and seuerall ioynts of its bodie," and then hurled cat and chopped-up corpse into the sea. The result was a great storm that one of the witches, under torture, declared would have drowned the king "if his faith had not preuailed aboue their ententions."

Acknowledgments

My deep thanks to the following journals and anthologies:

"Youth," Poets.org

"In Which a Spider Weaves a Web on My Computer Screen," *Everyman Pocket Poets Anthology: Buzzwords: Poems about Insects*

"'refugee'" *Tusculum Review*

"Not-Her," *The Progressive*

"Up the Hill," *Tusculum Review*

"A Dictator Walks into a Bar," *The Common*

"Fly," *The Washington Post*

"Dead Me, Live Me," *Raritan*

"Migration," *Raritan*

"False Teeth," *The Threepenny Review* and reprinted in *The Pushcart Prize: Best of the Small Presses*

"Words from Chernobyl," *Tusculum Review*

"What I Can Say in 2021 About a Famine in 2011," *Poetry Review* (London)

"Clearance," *Poetry Review* (London)

"Last Cigarette," *The Common*

"Apology to My Daughter," *The Common*

"Breaker," *Harvard Review*

"Ostrich" (under the title "Heat"), *The Southern Review*

"At Yeats's Tower," *The Southern Review*

"Stethoscope," *Poetry* and reprinted in *The Pushcart Prize: Best of the Small Presses*

"A Man Plays Debussy for a Blind, Eighty-Four-Year-Old Female Elephant," *The Southern Review*

"My Mother as the Eyes of a Whale on Her Ninety-Second Birthday," *Battery Journal*

"Conversation," *The Threepenny Review*

"For My Mother's Ninety-Sixth Birthday," *Harvard Review*

"The King's Touch," *Tusculum Review*

"Age of Wonder," *Provincetown Arts*

For Sarah and for my mother, Rosamond Sleigh; my deep thanks to Alan, David, Josh, Michael, and Patrick; and in memory of Mark Strand and Phil Levine.

TOM SLEIGH's many books of poetry include *House of Fact, House of Ruin*; *Station Zed*; *Army Cats*, winner of the John Updike Award from the American Academy of Arts and Letters; and *Space Walk*, which received the Kingsley Tufts Poetry Award. In addition, *Far Side of the Earth* won an Academy Award from the American Academy of Arts and Letters, *The Dreamhouse* was a finalist for the *Los Angeles Times* Book Prize, and *The Chain* was a finalist for the Lenore Marshall Poetry Prize. Sleigh is also the author of two books of essays, *The Land between Two Rivers: Writing in an Age of Refugees* and *Interview with a Ghost*. He has received the Poetry Society of America's Shelley Prize, and fellowships from the Guggenheim Foundation, two from the National Endowment for the Arts, and many other awards. His work appears in the *New Yorker* and *Poetry*, as well as in *The Best of the Best American Poetry*, *The Best American Travel Writing*, and *The Pushcart Prize Anthology*. He is a distinguished professor at Hunter College and has worked as a journalist in the Middle East and Africa. Sleigh lives in New York.

The text of *The King's Touch* is set in Adobe Garamond Pro.
Design and composition by Bookmobile Design & Digital
Publisher Services, Minneapolis, Minnesota.
Manufactured by McNaughton & Gunn on acid-free,
100 percent postconsumer wastepaper.